little book of

Southern-Style
Bites & Sips

little book of
Southern-Style Bites & Sips

delicious recipes for good time gatherings

Barbara Scott-Goodman

illustrations by Lindsey Spinks

Bluestreak
BOOKS

Bluestreak Books is an imprint of Weldon Owen,
a Bonnier Publishing USA company
www.bonnierpublishingusa.com

Library of Congress Cataloging in Publication data is available.
ISBN 978-168188-437-0

First Printed in 2018
10 9 8 7 6 5 4 3 2 1
2015 2016 2017 2018

Printed in China

Text and recipes by Barbara Scott-Goodman
Design by Barbara Scott-Goodman
Illustrations by Lindsey Spinks

CONTENTS

introduction

Introduction

S outherners are well-known for their love of entertaining and celebrating good times. They believe that gatherings that bring great food and friends together enhance our lives and make our long workdays worthwhile—hence the term "Southern Hospitality."

Because of the warm climate and long months of pleasant weather in the South, outdoor parties are always popular. Whether it's an afternoon barbecue on the lawn, a picnic lunch near the water, a cocktail party on the patio, or an impromptu potluck supper on the porch—friends and neighbors love to join in and enjoy the party.

There are a number of Southern dishes that are tailor-made for both indoor and outdoor entertaining and this little book features many of them. Included are classic recipes for luscious cheese straws, Cheddar and pecan wafers, pimiento cheese, and hot crab dip and culinary treasures such as Oysters Rockefeller, crab cakes, and fried chicken bites. In addition to cocktail fare, there are recipes for iconic Southern cocktails like Mint Juleps, Sazeracs, and punch as well as refreshing homemade lemonade and iced tea—all crafted for delicious leisurely sipping. These cherished recipes have been handed down through generations and are always on the party menu.

So sit back, relax, and savor a little taste of the South.

Cheers!

Small Bites

In the South, specialties such as cheese straws, Cheddar cheese and pecan wafers, and homemade pickles are among the many tasty small bites that are often served with cocktails, wine, and beer. These little snacks are easy to prepare, and they're always a welcome addition to a party.

✸✸✸✸✸✸✸

Spiced Pecans

Hot & Sweet Peanuts

Cheese Straws

Cheddar & Pecan Wafers

Southern-Style Deviled Eggs

Roasted Figs & Bacon

Eggplant Chips

Marinated Mushrooms

Quick Pickles

Spiced Pecans

Pecans are native to the South, where the climate provides a long, warm growing season. Bowls of fragrant roasted pecans always appear at Southerners' parties, especially around the holidays.

Makes about 4 cups

4 cups whole pecans

2 teaspoons kosher salt

Freshly ground black pepper

¼ teaspoon cayenne pepper

1 teaspoon dark brown sugar

1½ teaspoons chopped fresh rosemary leaves

1½ teaspoons chopped fresh thyme

1 tablespoon melted butter

2 tablespoons olive oil

1. Preheat the oven to 350°F.

2. Spread the pecans on a rimmed baking sheet and bake for 15 minutes. Remove from the oven and transfer to a bowl. Add 1 teaspoon of the salt, black pepper to taste, the cayenne, sugar, rosemary, thyme, butter, and oil and toss together until thoroughly coated. Return the pecans to the baking sheet and bake for another 2 to 3 minutes until toasted and fragrant. Be careful not to overcook them.

3. Let the pecans cool for a few minutes. Sprinkle with the remaining teaspoon of salt and let cool completely.

MAKE AHEAD:
The pecans will keep in an airtight container for up to 2 weeks.

Hot & Sweet Peanuts

These peanuts are a tasty and addictive snack, and go well with an ice-cold beer.

Makes about 3 cups

1 tablespoon olive oil
2 teaspoons chili powder
2 teaspoons ground cumin
2 teaspoons sugar
½ teaspoon cayenne
  pepper
3 cups unsalted peanuts
Kosher salt, for sprinkling

1. Preheat oven to 300°F.

2. Heat the oil in large skillet over medium heat. Add chili powder, cumin, sugar, and cayenne and stir until fragrant, about 30 seconds. Add the peanuts and stir until coated. Using a slotted spoon, transfer the peanuts to a large rimmed baking sheet.

3. Bake the peanuts, stirring and shaking the pan occasionally, until golden brown and fragrant, about 15 minutes. Transfer the peanuts another baking sheet lined with paper towels, sprinkle with salt to taste, and let cool.

MAKE AHEAD:
The peanuts will keep in an airtight container for up to 1 week.

Cheese Straws

Cheese straws are traditional Southern snacks that have been served with drinks for generations. When making these delicate straws and any other appetizer that uses grated cheese, be sure to freshly grate the cheese; pre-shredded tends to clump together.

Makes about 30 straws; serves 6 to 8

4 ounces sharp Cheddar cheese, grated

4 tablespoons unsalted butter, softened and cut into pieces

¾ cup all-purpose flour, plus more for rolling

½ teaspoon kosher salt

½ teaspoon cayenne pepper

1 tablespoon half-and-half

1. Preheat the oven to 350°F.

2. Put the cheese, butter, flour, salt, and cayenne pepper in the bowl of a food processor and pulse until the mixture resembles coarse crumbs. Add the half-and-half and process until the dough forms a ball.

3. On a lightly floured worked surface and using a lightly floured rolling pin, roll the dough out to a rectangle about 8 by 10 inches and ⅛-inch thick. Using a sharp knife or a pizza wheel, cut the dough into thin strips about 8 inches long by ⅓-inch wide. Gently transfer the strips to an ungreased baking sheet, spacing them about ¼ inch apart. Bake until the straws are lightly browned, 15 to 17 minutes. Let cool.

MAKE AHEAD:
Cheese straws will keep in an airtight container for up to 1 week.

Cheddar & Pecan Wafers

Here is another traditional appetizer that is key to Southern entertaining. These wafers are light bites to enjoy with a glass of wine or champagne.

Serves 6 to 8

4 ounces sharp Cheddar cheese, grated

½ cup unsalted butter, at room temperature

1 cup all-purpose flour

1 teaspoon kosher salt

¼ teaspoon black pepper

Pinch of cayenne pepper

30 pecan halves

2 egg whites, lightly beaten

1. Put the cheese, butter, flour, salt, black pepper, and cayenne pepper in the bowl of a food processor; process until a dough is formed, about 10 seconds. Turn dough out onto a work surface and divide into 2 equal pieces. Roll and shape each piece of dough into a 1½-inch-thick log; wrap with waxed or parchment paper and refrigerate until dough is firm, at least 2 hours and up to overnight.

2. Preheat oven to 350°F. Line two baking sheets with parchment paper and set aside.

3. Unwrap the dough and slice each log crosswise into ¼-inch-thick rounds. Place the rounds on the prepared baking sheets, spacing them about 1½ inches apart. Gently press a pecan half into the center of each round, then brush with the egg white.

4. Bake the wafers until crisp, about 15 minutes. Let the wafers cool for 5 minutes on the baking sheets, then transfer to a wire rack. Serve warm or at room temperature.

MAKE AHEAD:
The wafers will keep in an airtight container for up to 1 week.

Southern-Style Deviled Eggs

In the South, deviled eggs are often called "dressed eggs." The addition of sweet pickle relish makes these distinctly Southern.

Makes 1 dozen

6 large eggs

½ cup mayonnaise

1½ teaspoons sweet pickle relish

1 teaspoon Dijon mustard

½ teaspoon apple cider vinegar

¼ cup chopped fresh flat-leaf parsley

Kosher salt and freshly ground black pepper

Paprika, for garnish

1. Put the eggs in a single layer in a saucepan and add water to cover by 1½ inches. Bring to a boil over high heat. Cover the pan, reduce the heat to low, and cook for 1 minute. Remove from the heat and let stand, covered, for 14 minutes. Drain and rinse the eggs under cold water continuously for 1 minute.

2. Crack the egg shells and carefully peel them under cool running water. Gently dry with paper towels. Slice the eggs in half lengthwise, then carefully scoop out the yolks and put them in a bowl. Transfer the egg whites to a serving platter.

3. Mash the yolks using a fork. Add the mayonnaise, relish, mustard, vinegar, parsley, and salt and pepper to taste and mix well until smooth. Spoon the egg yolk mixture into the egg white halves. Sprinkle with paprika and serve.

MAKE AHEAD:
The deviled eggs may be refrigerated for up to 3 hours before serving.

Roasted Figs & Bacon

These sublime little snacks are easy to make and hit just the right notes of sweet, salty, and creamy.

Serves 6 to 8

6 smoked bacon slices

12 small ripe figs, halved

**Balsamic vinegar,
   for brushing**

½ cup crème fraîche

1. Preheat the oven to 350° F.

2. In a heavy skillet, arrange the bacon slices in a single layer and cook over low to medium-low heat, turning as needed, until just beginning to brown. Drain on paper towels. Cut each bacon slice into 4 to 6 pieces.

3. Arrange the figs on a baking sheet, cut sides up. Brush with balsamic vinegar and put a piece of bacon on each cut side. Bake until the figs are warmed, about 8 minutes. Top each fig with a spoonful of crème fraîche and serve.

Eggplant Chips

The key to making these crunchy chips is to continually replenish the bread crumbs while prepping the eggplant for frying, so they don't get soggy.

Serves 6 to 8

1 large eggplant, trimmed and peeled

1 large egg

1 cup whole milk

1½ cups all-purpose flour

3 cups fine fresh bread crumbs

Corn or canola oil, for frying

Kosher salt and freshly ground black pepper

1. Using a sharp knife, slice the eggplant into ¼-inch-thick sticks about 3 inches in length.

2. In a large bowl, whisk together the egg and milk and set aside.

3. Put the flour in a large lock-top plastic bag. Working in batches, add the eggplant pieces to the flour, seal the bag, and shake until they are well coated. Put the eggplant pieces in the bowl with the egg mixture and stir gently until they are completely coated.

4. Put about one-third of the bread crumbs on a plate. Dip the eggplant pieces into the crumbs, pressing hard so the crumbs stick. Shake gently to remove any excess. Repeat until all of the eggplant is coated, discarding the bread crumbs as they become wet and replacing with dry crumbs as needed.

5. Pour oil into a heavy-bottomed frying pan to a depth of 2 inches and heat until hot but not smoking. Add the eggplant, a handful at a time, and fry until golden brown, about 1 minute. Transfer to paper towels to drain. Sprinkle with salt and pepper to taste and serve at once.

Marinated Mushrooms

These aromatic mushrooms make an elegant little cocktail bite. Seek out small white mushrooms that are uniform in size.

Serves 6 to 8

¾ cup olive oil

½ cup water

¼ cup red wine vinegar

Juice of 1 lemon

1 tablespoon dry sherry

3 cloves garlic

2 tablespoons ground coriander seeds

1 tablespoon herbes de Provençe

2 teaspoons fennel seeds

½ teaspoon dried thyme

2 bay leaves

Kosher salt and freshly ground black pepper

1½ pounds small white mushrooms, rinsed and patted dry

1. Mix together the oil, water, vinegar, lemon juice, sherry, garlic, coriander, herbes de Provençe, fennel seeds, thyme, bay leaves, and salt and pepper in a large stockpot. Bring the mixture to a boil over medium-high heat, then reduce the heat to low and simmer for 10 minutes.

2. Add the mushrooms to the pot, stirring to coat them with sauce. Remove the pot from the heat and let the mushrooms marinate for 1 hour. Transfer to a container, cover and refrigerate for at least 2 hours or overnight.

3. To serve, transfer the mushrooms to a serving dish, using a slotted spoon. Pour a bit of the marinade over the them. Serve chilled or at room temperature with toothpicks.

MAKE AHEAD:

The mushrooms will keep, covered, in the refrigerator for up to 1 week.

Quick Pickles

Crisp and tangy pickled vegetables add vibrant crunch and color to a cocktail spread. Use any fresh vegetables of your choice.

Makes 2 pint-sized jars

1 pound fresh vegetables, such as carrots, cauliflower, cucumbers, green beans, or cherry tomatoes

2 cloves garlic, thinly sliced

8 sprigs fresh herbs, such as thyme, dill, or rosemary

1 teaspoon dried herbs

1 teaspoon each whole peppercorns, coriander, and mustard seeds

Pickling liquid:

1 cup white or apple cider vinegar

1 cup water

1 tablespoon kosher salt

1 tablespoon sugar

1. Thoroughly wash 2 wide-mouth pint jars, lids, and rings in the dishwasher or in warm soapy water. Rinse well and make sure that they are completely dry.

2. Rinse and pat the vegetables dry with paper towels. Peel, if necessary, and trim into desired shapes and sizes.

3. Divide the garlic, fresh and dried herbs, and peppercorns evenly among the jars. Pack in the vegetables snugly, but don't crowd them, leaving a ½ inch space from the rim of the jar.

4. To make the pickling liquid: Combine the vinegar, water, salt, and sugar in a small saucepan and bring to a boil over high heat, stirring to dissolve the salt and sugar. Remove from the heat.

5. Pour the pickling liquid over the vegetables, filling each jar to within a ½ inch from the top. Gently tap the jars a few times to remove any air bubbles. Cover tightly with the lids and rings and let cool. Refrigerate for at least 2 days before serving.

MAKE AHEAD:
The pickled vegetables will keep, covered, in the refrigerator for up to 2 months.

Spreads, Dips, Salsas & Relishes

*H*omemade dips and spreads like creamy hot crab dip and classic pimiento cheese are always on the table at Southerners' parties. They are excellent for spooning over warm bread and crackers. Add some piquant salsas and relishes made with garden-fresh fruit and vegetables to bring bold and bright flavors to your menu.

※※※※※※※※※※※

✻✻✻✻✻✻✻✻✻✻✻

Pimiento Cheese

Zesty Pimiento Cheese

Hot Crab Dip

Fresh Clam Dip

Grilled Corn Salsa

Spicy Peach Salsa

Green Tomato & Peach Relish

Green Tomato Chow-Chow

✻✻✻✻✻✻✻✻✻✻✻

Pimiento Cheese

Pimiento cheese is a staple of Southern kitchens. There are many versions of this all-time classic, but the main ingredients are sharp Cheddar cheese, mayonnaise, and pimientos. At cocktail parties, it is often served as a spread for crackers (Ritz are a favorite), chips, and celery.

Makes about 2½ cups; serves 6 to 8

1 (2 ounce) jar chopped pimientos

8 ounces sharp Cheddar cheese, grated

½ cup mayonnaise

1 tablespoon finely chopped yellow onion

1 clove garlic, finely minced

Dash of hot sauce

1 teaspoon Worcestershire sauce

1 teaspoon Dijon mustard

Ritz crackers, for serving

1. Drain the pimientos and reserve 1 tablespoon of the brine.

2. Pulse the cheese, reserved brine, mayonnaise, onion, and garlic in a food processor just until the mixture is combined and spreadable. Add the pimientos and pulse just to combine. Add the hot sauce, Worcestershire sauce, and mustard and pulse again. Taste and adjust the seasoning, if necessary.

3. Transfer to a medium bowl, cover, and refrigerate for 2 or 3 hours. Serve at room temperature with the crackers.

MAKE AHEAD:

Pimiento cheese will keep, covered, in the refrigerator for up to 1 week.

Zesty Pimiento Cheese

This hot and spicy version of pimiento cheese makes a flavorful spread, as well as a scrumptious filling for a Southern-style grilled cheese sandwich.

Makes about 2½ cups; serves 6 to 8

8 ounces sharp Cheddar cheese, grated

½ cup mayonnaise

2 tablespoons finely chopped pickled jalapeños, plus ½ teaspoon brine

2 tablespoons drained and finely chopped pimientos

1 tablespoon minced green onion (white part only)

1 teaspoon minced chipotle pepper

1 teaspoon fresh lime juice

½ teaspoon Worcestershire sauce

Crackers or flatbread, for serving

1. Put the cheese, mayonnaise, jalapeños and brine, pimientos, green onion, pepper, lime juice, and Worcestershire sauce in a large bowl and mix together.

2. Cover and refrigerate for 2 to 3 hours before serving. Serve at room temperature with crackers.

Hot Crab Dip

Served with crackers and tortilla chips, this rich and creamy hot dip is a Southern classic and is always a big hit.

Serves 6 to 8

1 package (8 ounces) cream cheese, at room temperature

½ cup mayonnaise

½ cup sour cream

1 cup grated Parmesan cheese, divided

1 cup grated Cheddar cheese

1 tablespoon fresh lemon juice

1 teaspoon hot sauce

1 pound lump crab meat, drained and picked over

Kosher salt and freshly ground black pepper

2 green onions (white and green parts), minced

Crackers or tortilla chips, for serving

1. Preheat oven to 400°F.

2. In a large bowl, using an electric mixer on medium speed, blend the cream cheese, mayonnaise, and sour cream together until smooth. Add ½ cup of the Parmesan cheese, the Cheddar cheese, lemon juice, and hot sauce and stir until well combined. Fold in the crab meat and add salt and pepper to taste. Spoon the mixture into a 1-quart baking dish and sprinkle with the remaining ½ cup Parmesan cheese.

3. Bake until bubbly and hot, 25 to 35 minutes. Remove from the oven, garnish with green onions, and serve.

Fresh Clam Dip

Everyone loves this easy-to-make, zesty clam dip. Serve it slightly chilled with pita crisps and garden-fresh vegetables. It's also very good stuffed into celery and topped with chopped black olives.

Serves 6 to 8

12 cherrystone clams, well rinsed

1 package (8 ounces) cream cheese, at room temperature

½ cup low-fat sour cream

½ red bell pepper, seeded and finely diced

1 teaspoon celery seed

1 to 2 teaspoons hot sauce

Kosher salt

1. Put the clams in a large soup pot, add 2 cups of water and bring to a boil. Cover and cook until the clams open, about 5 minutes. Drain and let cool. When cool enough to handle, remove the clams from their shells, coarsely chop, and set aside.

2. Put the clams, cream cheese, sour cream, pepper, celery seed, hot sauce, and salt to taste in the bowl of a food processor. Pulse until finely chopped but not too smooth. Taste and adjust the seasonings and pulse again briefly. Scrape the dip into a bowl, cover, and chill for a few hours before serving.

MAKE AHEAD:
The dip will keep, covered, in the refrigerator for up to 3 days.

Grilled Corn Salsa

This smoky-flavored salsa is a great dip for tortilla chips, and can also be served with grilled salmon or steak. For the best flavor grill the corn over a charcoal fire.

Makes about 2 cups; serves 6 to 8

3 large ears fresh corn, husks on

½ cup diced red onion

2 ripe tomatoes, diced

1 serrano or jalapeño pepper, seeded and minced

Juice of 1 lime

½ teaspoon ground chili powder

½ teaspoon ground cumin

½ cup chopped fresh cilantro

Kosher salt and freshly ground black pepper

1. Prepare a charcoal grill.

2. Grill the corn, turning as needed, over medium-high heat until the husks are evenly charred. Take the corn off the grill. Remove the husks and silk, return the corn to the grill and cook, turning as needed, until nicely charred, 2 to 3 minutes. Let cool for a few minutes.

3. Cut the corn off the cobs and place in a large bowl. Add the onion, tomatoes, pepper, lime juice, chili powder, cumin, cilantro, and salt and pepper to taste. Taste and adjust seasonings, if necessary. Serve at once.

Spicy Peach Salsa

This versatile salsa is both sweet and spicy. It is a delicious dip to serve with chips or bread, and makes a terrific condiment for grilled burgers and hot dogs, or tacos.

Makes 1½ cups

1 tablespoon olive oil

6 cloves garlic, thinly sliced

8 shallots, peeled and thinly sliced

1 cup dry white wine

4 large peaches, peeled, pitted, and cut into ½-inch-thick wedges

2 plum tomatoes, cut into ½-inch-thick wedges

½ cup firmly packed dark brown sugar

1 tablespoon low-sodium soy sauce

½ teaspoon red pepper flakes

Dash of hot sauce

1. Heat the oil in a large sauté pan over medium heat. Add the garlic and shallots and cook for about 3 minutes until softened and golden. Add the wine, bring to a boil, then reduce the heat and simmer, uncovered, for 15 minutes. Add the peaches, tomatoes, brown sugar, soy sauce, pepper flakes, and hot sauce to the pan and bring to a boil over high heat. Reduce the heat to medium and cook for 20 minutes, stirring frequently. The peaches and tomatoes should be broken down but remain fairly chunky. Taste and adjust the seasonings, if necessary.

2. Serve the salsa warm, at room temperature, or chilled. It will keep, covered, in the refrigerator for 3 days.

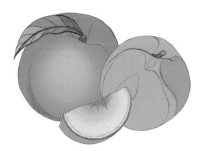

Green Tomato & Peach Relish

This is a lovely relish made with ripe—but not too ripe—green tomatoes, peaches, and a well-charred Vidalia onion.

Makes about 2 cups

½ large Vidalia onion, cut into thick slices

2 large firm green tomatoes, cut into ½-inch dice

1 ripe peach, peeled, pitted, and cut into ¼-inch dice

½ lime, juiced and zested

1 jalapeño pepper, peeled, seeded, and diced

2 green onions (white and green parts), minced

1 knob (about 1 inch) fresh ginger, peeled and grated

2 tablespoons extra-virgin olive oil

½ cup chopped fresh flat-leaf parsley

¼ cup minced fresh chives

Kosher salt and freshly ground black pepper

1. Prepare a charcoal or gas grill. Grill the onion slices, turning once, over medium heat, until blackened and charred, 3 to 4 minutes per side. (Alternatively, preheat the broiler and broil the onion slices until blackened and charred.) When cool enough to handle, coarsely chop the onions and transfer to a large bowl.

2. Add the tomatoes, peach, lime juice and zest, jalapeño, green onions, and ginger and toss to mix. Add the oil, parsley, chives, and salt and pepper to taste and toss again. Taste and adjust the seasonings, if necessary. Cover and refrigerate for up to 3 hours before serving. The relish will keep, covered, in the refrigerator for up to 1 week.

Green Tomato Chow-Chow

Green tomatoes have a nice, bright, slightly acidic flavor and they hold up well when pickled or stewed. The origins of the word "chow-chow" are obscure; it is simply a type of pickled relish that is most often served cold. Try it alongside Slow-Cooked Chicken Wings (page 48).

Makes 2½ pints

- 6 green tomatoes, cored and finely chopped
- 2 green bell peppers, seeded and finely chopped
- 1 red bell pepper, seeded and finely chopped
- 2 onions, finely chopped
- 1 tablespoon yellow mustard seeds
- 1½ teaspoons celery seeds
- 1 cup apple cider vinegar
- 1 cup sugar
- 1 tablespoon kosher salt

1. Put the tomatoes, peppers, onions, mustard seeds, celery seeds, vinegar, sugar, and salt in a large nonreactive pot, stir well, and bring to a boil over medium-high heat. Reduce the heat to low and simmer for 25 minutes. Let cool.

2. Transfer the chow-chow to clean glass containers. It will keep, covered, in the refrigerator for up to a month.

Seafood

Seafood is a very important element in Southern cooking. Fresh oysters, shrimp, crab, and a wide variety of fish are abundant throughout the region and are featured in a number of classic dishes. Here are some Southern-style recipes that are sure to be a big hit with your guests.

※※※※※※※※※※※※

❋❋❋❋❋❋❋❋❋❋

Oysters Rockefeller

Pickled Oysters

Shrimp Cocktail

Grilled Shrimp Cocktail

Pickled Shrimp

Crabmeat Toasts

Crab Cake Sliders

Smoked Salmon Mousse

Seafood Sauces

❋❋❋❋❋❋❋❋❋❋

Oysters Rockefeller

The original recipe for oysters Rockefeller was created at Antoine's Restaurant in New Orleans in 1899, and the recipe has always been kept a secret. It is believed that the recipe was originally made with watercress instead of spinach and a dash of absinthe in place of Pernod. But no matter how you make this Southern classic, it is certainly "rich as Rockefeller."

Serves 6 to 8

2 cups loosely packed fresh spinach

1 bunch watercress, stems trimmed

1 clove garlic, thinly sliced

½ cup chopped green onion (white parts only)

¾ cup unsalted butter, at room temperature

½ cup dry bread crumbs

2 tablespoons Pernod

1 teaspoon hot sauce

Kosher salt and freshly ground black pepper

1 pound rock salt

24 fresh oysters, shucked, bottom shells reserved

¼ cup freshly grated Parmesan cheese

Lemon wedges, for serving

1. Position a rack in the top third of oven and preheat to 450°F.

2. Put the spinach, watercress, garlic, and green onion in the bowl of a food processor. Pulse until the mixture is finely chopped. Transfer to a bowl.

3. Combine the butter, bread crumbs, Pernod, and hot sauce in the food processor. Process until well blended. Add the spinach mixture and salt and pepper to taste and pulse until just blended.

4. Sprinkle rock salt over a large rimmed baking sheet about ½-inch deep. Arrange the oysters in half shells on the rock salt. Top each oyster with 1 tablespoon of the spinach mixture. Sprinkle with the cheese. Bake until spinach mixture browns on top, 6 to 8 minutes.

5. Serve warm with lemon wedges.

MAKE AHEAD:
The spinach mixture can be made up to 8 hours ahead. Cover and refrigerate until ready to use.

Pickled Oysters

Pickled oysters served on grilled bread and topped with arugula make a fantastic appetizer.

Makes about 1 quart

Pickling Spice:

1 teaspoon black peppercorns

1 teaspoon coriander seeds

½ teaspoon red pepper flakes

1 bay leaf

1 cinnamon stick, halved

1 whole clove

½ cup packed light brown sugar

¼ cup kosher salt

1 teaspoon mustard seeds

2 cups white wine vinegar

½ cup water

2 tablespoons Worcestershire sauce

30 large, meaty oysters, shucked

1 lemon, thinly sliced

1 white onion, thinly sliced

Grilled country bread, for serving

Fresh lemon juice, for serving

2 cups chopped arugula for serving

1. To make the pickling spice: Put the peppercorns, coriander seeds, pepper flakes, bay leaf, and cinnamon stick in a small bowl and stir together. Transfer to a large saucepan and add the brown sugar, salt, mustard seeds, vinegar, water, and Worcestershire sauce. Bring to a boil over high heat, then boil, stirring occasionally, until the salt and sugar dissolve. Set aside.

2. Bring a pot of salted water to a boil. Add the oysters and cook for 1 minute; drain.

3. Layer the oysters, lemon, and onion in a large clean jar with a lid. Pour the pickling liquid over them. Cover and refrigerate overnight before serving.

4. To serve, drain the oysters and arrange over pieces of grilled bread. Sprinkle with a bit of lemon juice, top with arugula, and serve.

MAKE AHEAD:

The oysters will keep, covered, in the refrigerator for up to 1 month.

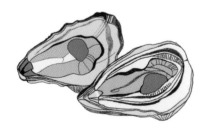

Shrimp Cocktail

Shrimp cocktail is always a crowd-pleaser—you can never go wrong when you serve it at a party. Although it is easier to buy shrimp that is already shelled and deveined, they taste much better when cooked with their shells on.

Serves 6 to 8

1 small onion

1 lemon, cut in half crosswise

2 cloves garlic

2 sprigs fresh tarragon

1 tablespoon Old Bay seasoning

1 teaspoon kosher salt

1 teaspoon whole black peppercorns

1 bay leaf

2 pounds extra-large or jumbo shrimp, unpeeled

Cocktail Sauce:

½ cup ketchup

¼ cup chili sauce

¼ cup prepared horseradish

1 teaspoon fresh lemon juice

1 teaspoon Worcestershire sauce

2 dashes of hot sauce

Lemon wedges, for garnish

1. Put the onion, lemon, garlic, tarragon, Old Bay seasoning, salt, peppercorns, and bay leaf in a large pot of water and bring to a boil over high heat. Reduce the heat to low and simmer for about 15 minutes. Bring the poaching liquid back to a rapid boil over high heat. Add the shrimp and cook until they are bright pink on the outside, 3 to 5 minutes. Drain and transfer the shrimp to a bowl of ice water. Drain again. Peel and devein the shrimp, leaving the tails intact. Refrigerate the shrimp until serving.

2. To make the cocktail sauce: Whisk together the ketchup, chili sauce, horseradish, lemon juice, Worcestershire sauce, and hot sauce in a bowl. Cover and refrigerate until chilled, about 20 minutes.

3. Serve the shrimp on a bed of ice garnished with lemon wedges and the cocktail sauce on the side for dipping.

MAKE AHEAD:

The shrimp will keep covered, in the refrigerator for up to 1 day. The cocktail sauce will keep, covered, in the refrigerator up to 2 days. Stir well before serving.

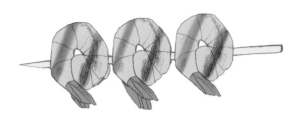

Grilled Shrimp Cocktail

Here is a grilled version of shrimp cocktail. Although it is delicious with classic Cocktail Sauce (page 36) or Remoulade Sauce (page 45), Lemon-Paprika Aioli complements the smoky shrimp beautifully.

Serves 6 to 8

1 pound large shrimp, peeled and deveined

2 tablespoons olive oil

1 tablespoon minced garlic

1 teaspoon kosher salt

Lemon-Paprika Aioli:

2 egg yolks

1 clove garlic, finely minced

2 tablespoons fresh lemon juice

1 cup corn oil

1 teaspoon smoked paprika

Pinch of cayenne pepper

Kosher salt and freshly ground black pepper

1. Soak 8 wooden skewers in water for at least 1 hour. Thread 3 shrimp onto each skewer and transfer to a baking dish.

2. In a small bowl, whisk together the olive oil, garlic, and salt. Brush the shrimp with the olive oil mixture, cover with plastic wrap, and refrigerate for 30 minutes.

3. Prepare a gas or charcoal grill. Grill the shrimp, turning once, over medium heat until firm to the touch and slightly charred, 2 to 3 minutes per side.

4. To make the Lemon-Paprika Aioli: Put the egg yolks, garlic, and lemon juice in a food processor and pulse until blended. Gradually add the corn oil in a thin stream, with the machine still running, until smooth and thickened. Add the paprika, cayenne, and salt and black pepper to taste and pulse again. Transfer to a bowl. The sauce will keep, covered, in the refrigerator, for up to 2 days.

Pickled Shrimp

This Southern-inspired appetizer is a favorite for serving with drinks before dinner or as part of a cocktail party buffet. Pickled shrimp should be made ahead of time, since they taste even better after a few days of marinating.

Serves 6 to 8

Pickling Mix:

1 cup tarragon vinegar

6 slices fresh ginger

2 tablespoons coriander seeds

1 tablespoon fennel seeds

1 tablespoon mixed peppercorns

2½ pounds large shrimp

1 red onion, thinly sliced

1 lemon, thinly sliced

¼ cup small capers, drained

3 cloves garlic, thinly sliced

Pinch of cayenne pepper

4 bay leaves

¾ cup extra-virgin olive oil

Kosher salt and freshly ground black pepper

1. To make the pickling mix: Combine the vinegar, ½ cup water, ginger, coriander and fennel seeds, and peppercorns in a medium, nonreactive saucepan. Bring to a boil over medium-high heat. Reduce the heat to low and simmer for 10 minutes. Remove from the heat.

2. Bring a large pot of salted water to a boil over high heat. Add the shrimp. Remove the pot from the heat and let stand until the shrimp turn pink, about 3 minutes. Drain, rinse, and let cool, then shell and devein the shrimp.

3. Put the shrimp in a large bowl with the onion, lemon slices, capers, garlic, cayenne, and bay leaves and gently toss together. Whisk the oil and salt and pepper to taste into the pickling mixture and pour over the shrimp. Transfer the mixture to a clean glass jar or container with a lid. Cover tightly and refrigerate for at least 24 hours or up to 3 days.

4. To serve the shrimp, use a slotted spoon to transfer them to a platter and serve cold or at room temperature with toothpicks.

Crabmeat Toasts

Crabmeat salad, made with fresh jumbo lump crab, is a luxurious treat. Whether you spread it over toast points or Ritz crackers, or spoon it into endive leaves, it's delicious to snack on with a cocktail.

Serves 6 to 8

- 1 pound jumbo lump crabmeat, drained and picked over
- 1 rib celery, trimmed and cut into small dice
- ¼ cup diced red onion
- 4 teaspoons minced fresh chives, plus more for garnish
- 1 teaspoon minced fresh tarragon leaves
- ⅓ cup mayonnaise
- 3 tablespoons sour cream
- 1 teaspoon fresh lemon juice
- ½ teaspoon Dijon mustard
- Kosher salt and freshly ground black pepper
- Toast points or crackers, for serving

1. In a medium bowl, toss together the crabmeat, celery, chives, and tarragon.

2. In a small bowl, stir together the mayonnaise, sour cream, lemon juice, and mustard. Fold into the crabmeat mixture until just coated. Add salt and pepper to taste.

3. Spread the crabmeat salad over toast points or Ritz crackers, garnish with chives, and serve.

MAKE AHEAD:
The crabmeat salad will keep, covered, for up to 8 hours.

Crab Cake Sliders

This is the right mix of ingredients for a great-tasting crab cake that's more crabmeat than bread crumbs. Refrigerate the crab cakes for at least an hour before they're cooked so that they hold together.

Makes 12 sliders; serves 6 to 8

1 pound lump crabmeat, drained and picked over

1 tablespoon fresh lemon juice

½ cup plain bread crumbs

1 large egg

5 tablespoons mayonnaise

2 green onions (white and green parts), finely minced

1 tablespoon chopped fresh flat-leaf parsley

1 tablespoon dry mustard

Kosher salt and freshly ground black pepper

1. Put the crabmeat in a bowl, sprinkle with the lemon juice, and gently toss.

2. In a large bowl, mix together the bread crumbs, egg, mayonnaise, green onions, parsley, mustard, and salt and pepper to taste. Add the crabmeat and mix together gently.

3. Using your hands, shape the mixture into 12 small patties, about 1-inch thick and 2 inches wide, and transfer to a baking sheet. Cover with plastic wrap and refrigerate for at least 1 hour.

2 tablespoons unsalted
butter

2 tablespoons canola
or safflower oil

Spicy Tartar Sauce
(page 44)

12 slider rolls, split

2 cups mixed
salad greens

4. Heat 1 tablespoon each of the butter and oil in a large skillet over medium heat and cook half of the crab cakes, turning once, until golden, 3 to 5 minutes per side. Drain on paper towels. Heat the remaining butter and oil and repeat with the remaining crab cakes.

5. To assemble the sliders, put a crab cake on each roll bottom. Top with the tartar sauce, the greens, and roll tops, and serve at once.

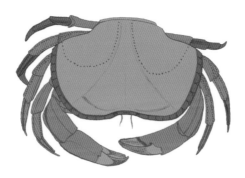

Smoked Salmon Mousse

Here is a very simple and delicious spread to prepare in the food processor. Although you can serve it right away, it tastes better after a day of chilling in the refrigerator. Aquavit, the caraway-flavored Scandinavian spirit, adds an extra dash of flavor to the mousse.

Serves 6 to 8

1 package (8 ounces) cream cheese, at room temperature

4 ounces smoked salmon

⅓ cup chopped green onions

2 tablespoons fresh lemon juice

2 tablespoons Aquavit

Dash of hot sauce

Freshly ground black pepper

Chopped red onion, for garnish

Drained capers, for garnish

Rye toast or crackers, for serving

1. Put the cream cheese, salmon, onions, lemon juice, Aquavit, hot sauce, and pepper to taste in the bowl of a food processor and process until very smooth. Transfer the mixture to a container, cover and refrigerate for up to 1 day.

2. Garnish with chopped onion and capers, then serve with toast or crackers.

Seafood Sauces

Here are some flavor-packed sauces made with homemade mayonnaise that will complement any number of seafood dishes. Mayo from scratch is easy to make with a food processor and a few room-temperature ingredients. The trick is to add the oils in a slow, steady stream so the ingredients emulsify into a silken sauce.

Herbed Tartar Sauce

Makes about 1¼ cups

Homemade Mayonnaise:

1 large egg, at room temperature

1 tablespoon fresh lemon juice

1 teaspoon Dijon mustard

Pinch of salt

1 large egg

Dash of hot sauce

¼ cup safflower oil

¼ cup olive oil

2 tablespoons finely diced dill pickle

1 tablespoon small capers, drained

1 tablespoon chopped fresh flat-leaf parsley

1 tablespoon minced fresh chives

1 tablespoon minced fresh tarragon leaves

Freshly ground black pepper

1. Put the egg, lemon juice, mustard, salt, and hot sauce in the bowl of a food processor and process until smooth. With the motor running, slowly pour the oils in a steady stream through the feed tube. When thoroughly blended, turn off the machine, scrape down the sides and taste and adjust the seasonings, if necessary. Scrape into a container, cover, and refrigerate for up to 5 days.

2. About 1 hour before serving, fold the pickle, capers, parsley, chives, and tarragon into the mayonnaise. Season with pepper to taste. Cover and refrigerate until serving.

NOTE:

If you have any concern regarding the use of raw egg in homemade mayonnaise, use good-quality store-bought mayonnaise instead.

Spicy Tartar Sauce

Makes about 1 1/4 cups

1 cup mayonnaise, homemade (page 43), or good-quality store-bought mayonnaise

1/4 cup sweet pickle relish

2 tablespoons chopped fresh cilantro

2 tablespoons chopped fresh flat-leaf parsley

2 tablespoons fresh lime juice

1 tablespoon chili powder

1 tablespoon ground cumin

8 dashes hot sauce

Kosher salt and freshly ground black pepper

In a medium bowl, stir together the mayonnaise, relish, cilantro, parsley, lime juice, chili powder, cumin, hot sauce, and salt and pepper to taste. Cover and refrigerate until serving.

Remoulade Sauce

Makes about 1 cup

- ⅔ cup mayonnaise, homemade (page 43), or good-quality store-bought mayonnaise
- ¼ cup Dijon mustard
- 2 green onions (white and green parts), chopped
- 2 tablespoons finely minced fresh flat-leaf parsley
- 1 tablespoon sweet paprika
- 1 teaspoon fresh lemon juice
- 1 teaspoon Worcestershire sauce
- Dash of hot sauce
- Kosher salt and freshly ground black pepper

In a medium bowl, whisk together the mayonnaise, mustard, green onions, parsley, paprika, lemon juice, Worcestershire sauce, hot sauce, and salt and pepper to taste until well blended. Cover and refrigerate until serving.

MAKE AHEAD:

All of these sauces can be stored in the refrigerator for a day or two ahead of time. Bring to room temperature before serving.

Meat

Heartier party fare like slow-cooked chicken wings, meatballs, and ham biscuits pair deliciously with cocktails. When you're planning your party, make sure that a sampling of these savory appetizers are on the buffet table.

※※※※※※※※※※※

❋❋❋❋❋❋❋❋❋❋

Slow-Cooked Chicken Wings

Fried Chicken Bites

Chicken Salad & Endive

Chicken Liver Pâté

Cocktail Meatballs
with Sweet Barbecue Sauce

Biscuits with Ham & Fig Preserves

Homemade Barbecue Sauce

Alabama White Sauce

❋❋❋❋❋❋❋❋❋❋

Slow-Cooked Chicken Wings

These wings marinate in a spicy rub before being slow cooked on the grill or in the oven. Serve them with Homemade Barbecue Sauce (page 56) or Alabama White Sauce (page 57), or both!

Serves 6 to 8

Dry Rub:

2 tablespoons garlic powder

2 tablespoons light brown sugar

1 tablespoon onion powder

1 tablespoon dried oregano

1 tablespoon kosher salt

1 tablespoon freshly ground black pepper

1 teaspoon cayenne pepper

4 pounds chicken wings

Extra-virgin olive oil, for serving

Sea salt

1. To make the dry rub: Mix together the garlic powder, brown sugar, onion powder, oregano, salt, black pepper, and cayenne pepper in a large bowl. Add the chicken wings and stir and turn to coat well. Cover and let marinate in the refrigerator for at least 2 hours or overnight.

2. To grill the wings: Preheat a gas grill or prepare a charcoal fire for indirect, medium-low heat. Put the wings in the center of the grill grate over indirect heat. Cover and grill, turning the wings every 10 minutes, until they are slightly crispy and completely cooked through, 30 to 35 minutes.

3. To cook the wings in the oven: Preheat the oven to 375°F. Arrange the wings on a roasting rack set over a rimmed baking sheet. Bake for 45 minutes, turning every 15 minutes. Remove the wings and preheat the broiler. Broil the wings until browned and crispy, 5 to 10 minutes.

4. Arrange the wings on a large platter. Brush with olive oil, sprinkle with sea salt, and serve with desired sauce (see note).

Fried Chicken Bites

Fried chicken is simplicity in itself, and this Southern staple has been served at picnics, parties, lunches, and dinners for many generations. These crispy bites taste great with a spritz of fresh lemon or a dip of Alabama White Sauce (page 57).

Serves 6 to 8

3 pounds skinless, boneless chicken breasts, cut into bite-size pieces

2 cups all-purpose flour

2 teaspoons kosher salt

2 teaspoons paprika

1 teaspoon cayenne pepper

1 teaspoon freshly ground black pepper

3 large eggs

2 tablespoons milk

Vegetable, canola, or peanut oil, for frying

Lemon wedges, for serving

1. Pat the chicken pieces dry and set aside.

2. In a shallow bowl, whisk together the flour, salt, paprika, cayenne pepper, and black pepper. In another shallow bowl, whisk together the eggs and milk.

3. Dredge the chicken pieces in the flour mixture, shake off the excess, then dredge in the egg mixture. Dredge once more in the flour mixture and shake off the excess.

4. Pour 2 inches of oil into a large heavy-bottomed skillet, preferably cast iron, and heat over medium-high heat until it registers 350°F on a deep-frying thermometer. Working in batches, fry the chicken, turning occasionally, until golden brown, about 4 minutes. With a slotted spoon, transfer the chicken to a baking sheet lined with paper towels and let drain a bit before serving.

5. Serve immediately with lemon wedges and a dipping sauce (see note), if using.

Chicken Salad & Endive

Succulent spears of endive filled with creamy chicken salad are perfect finger food. It's best to make the chicken salad a day ahead of time to give the flavors time to meld and intensify.

Makes about 3 dozen

About 4 pounds bone-in, skin-on chicken breasts

2 green onions, cut in half

¼ teaspoon black peppercorns

1. Fill a large heavy pot or Dutch oven about two-thirds full of water. Add the green onions and peppercorns, cover, and bring to a boil over high heat. Turn off the heat and slip the chicken pieces into the hot water. If needed, add boiling water to cover the chicken by 2 inches. Cover and let the chicken stand in the hot water for about 2 hours. Do not turn the heat back on. To test for doneness, cut into 1 piece of chicken and check the meat near the bone. If it is still pink, return the pot to low heat, bring the water to a simmer and cook 10 minutes more.

2. Using a slotted spoon, transfer the chicken to a bowl and let cool. Reserve the cooking liquid for broth, if desired. Remove and discard the bones, skin, and fat. Pat the meat dry with paper towels, cut or shred into small bite-size pieces, and transfer to a mixing bowl.

- ⅔ cup mayonnaise, homemade (page 43), or good-quality store-bought mayonnaise
- ¼ cup sour cream, plus more to taste
- 1 tablespoon fresh lemon juice
- ½ teaspoon sweet pickle brine (optional)
- 3 ribs celery, finely diced
- ½ cup finely diced red onion (optional)
- ½ cup walnut or pecan halves, finely chopped
- 3 tablespoons chopped fresh tarragon, parsley, or chives, plus more for garnish
- Kosher salt and freshly ground black pepper
- 3 heads Belgian endive, separated into leaves

3. In a small bowl, whisk together the mayonnaise, sour cream, and lemon juice. Whisk in the brine, if using. Pour over the chicken. Add the celery, onion (if using), nuts, herbs, and salt and pepper to taste. Toss gently but thoroughly. Cover and refrigerate for at least 4 hours. Taste and adjust the seasonings, if necessary.

4. To serve, spoon the chicken salad into the endive pieces, garnish with herbs, and arrange on a platter.

NOTE:

Other good garnishes for chicken salad include: chopped sweet pickles or pickled jalapeños, Kalamata olives, cherry tomatoes, slivered almonds or pistachios, and crumbled cooked bacon.

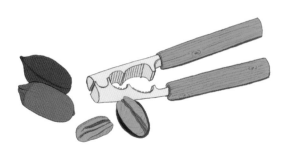

Chicken Liver Pâté

This is an easy chicken liver pâté that you can make well ahead of time. It's always delicious for any type of occasion.

Serves 6 to 8

2 tablespoons unsalted butter

¼ cup olive oil

1 cup chopped onions

3 cloves garlic, thinly sliced

1 pound chicken livers, trimmed, rinsed, and patted dry

½ cup chicken broth

½ cup dry white wine

2 teaspoons herbes de Provençe

2 tablespoons capers, drained

Kosher salt and freshly ground black pepper

1. Heat the butter and oil in a large skillet over medium heat. Add the onions and garlic and cook, stirring often, until softened, about 5 minutes. Add the chicken livers and cook, turning occasionally, until lightly browned, about 5 minutes. Add the broth, wine, and herbs and cook, stirring often, until the liquid has reduced by two-thirds, 4 to 5 minutes. Add the capers and cook for another minute.

2. Transfer the mixture to the bowl of a food processor, add salt and pepper to taste, and blend until smooth. Taste and adjust the seasonings, if necessary. Transfer to a bowl, cover, and refrigerate for at least 2 hours. Bring to room temperature before serving.

MAKE AHEAD:

The pâté will keep, covered, in the refrigerator for up to 1 week. Bring to room temperature before serving.

Cocktail Meatballs with Sweet Barbecue Sauce

Savory meatballs served with a warm sweet barbecue sauce have a great intense flavor. You can prep the meatballs and store them in the refrigerator for an hour or two before frying them.

Makes about 32 meatballs; serves 6 to 8

1 pound ground beef

½ pound ground pork

½ cup panko (Japanese bread crumbs)

½ cup freshly grated Parmesan cheese

1 large egg

2 cloves garlic, minced

Kosher salt and freshly ground black pepper

Corn or canola oil, for frying

Barbecue Sauce:

¼ cup light brown sugar

½ cup Homemade Barbecue Sauce (page 56), or good-quality store-bought barbecue sauce

Minced fresh chives, for garnish

1. In a large bowl, combine the beef, pork, panko, cheese, egg, garlic, and salt and pepper to taste until well combined. Using your hands, form into balls that are about 1-inch in diameter.

2. Heat 3 tablespoons of the oil in a large skillet over medium heat. Add the meatballs to the pan, in batches, and cook until brown on one side before turning, about 4 minutes per side. When cooked through, use a slotted spoon to transfer the meatballs to a baking sheet lined with paper towels. Repeat with the remaining meatballs, adding more oil as needed. Drain the pan, leaving a few tablespoons of fat.

3. To make the barbecue sauce: Return the pan to medium-high heat. Add 2 tablespoons of water to deglaze the pan, and stir, to scrape up the brown bits. Add the brown sugar, adding a little more water if it seems too dry. It should start to bubble and look like dark caramel. Remove from the heat, add the barbecue sauce, and stir well until the sugar has dissolved.

4. Arrange the meatballs in a shallow bowl, pour the warm sauce over them, garnish with chives, and serve with toothpicks.

Biscuits with Ham & Fig Preserves

It's hard to imagine Southern cooking without biscuits coming to mind. They are served with sausage and grits, fried chicken, as well as with sweet butter and jam. They are a perennial favorite for cocktail parties when served filled with slices of baked country ham. And there is nothing better to add to these succulent little sandwiches than a dollop of sweet fig preserves.

Serves 6 to 8

Biscuits:

2 cups all-purpose flour, plus more for dusting

2 tablespoons baking powder

1 tablespoon sugar

1 teaspoon salt

5 tablespoons cold, unsalted butter, cut into 5 pieces

1 cup whole milk

1. To make the biscuits: Preheat the oven to 425°F. Sift the flour, baking powder, sugar, and salt into a large mixing bowl. Transfer to the bowl of a food processor. Add the butter and pulse about 6 times until the mixture resembles rough crumbs. Return the dough to the bowl, add the milk and stir with a fork until the dough forms a rough ball.

2. Turn the dough out onto a well-floured surface and pat it into a rough rectangle about 1 inch thick. Fold it over and gently pat it down again. Repeat. Cover the dough loosely with a kitchen towel and let rest for 30 minutes.

3. Gently pat the dough into a rectangle roughly 10 by 6 inches. Using a biscuit cutter or a floured glass, cut the dough into biscuits, being careful not to twist the cutter.

4. Arrange the biscuits on a baking sheet and bake until golden brown, 10 to 15 minutes.

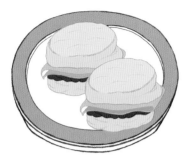

Fig Preserves:

3 allspice berries

1 cinnamon stick

2 whole cloves

2 large pieces
   orange peel

1 small knob of fresh
   ginger, peeled

1 pound fresh figs,
   trimmed and cut into
   small pieces

¼ cup dark brown sugar
   (or more to taste)

¼ cup orange juice

About 18 thin slices
   of country ham

5. To make the preserves: Put the allspice, cinnamon stick, cloves, orange peel, and ginger in a square of cheesecloth and tie it tightly with a piece of twine, making sure that one end of the twine is long enough to tie around the handle of a saucepan.

6. In a large saucepan, combine the figs, brown sugar, and orange juice. Add the spice bag to the pot, tying one end of the twine around the pot handle, and stir. Bring to a simmer over medium-low heat, then cook, stirring frequently, until the mixture thickens and bubbles begin to appear on the surface, 15 to 20 minutes.

7. Remove the spice bag and let the preserves cool in the pan. Transfer to a clean jar with a lid, cover, and refrigerate. The preserves will keep, covered, for about 2 weeks.

8. To serve, split the biscuits, spread with fig preserves, and stuff with ham.

Homemade Barbecue Sauce

This barbecue sauce has a complex range of flavors. It's very good to baste onto chicken or pork near the end of cooking on the grill. It also makes an excellent dipping sauce for chicken wings and ribs.

Makes about 2 cups

2 tablespoons corn oil

2 cloves garlic, thinly sliced

⅓ cup sliced onion

1½ cups ketchup

½ cup dark brown sugar

2 tablespoons Worcestershire sauce

Juice of ½ lemon

2 teaspoons chili powder

1 teaspoon Dijon mustard

1 teaspoon hot sauce

Heat the oil in a large saucepan over medium-low heat. Add the garlic and onion and cook, stirring, until golden, about 5 minutes. Add the ketchup, sugar, Worcestershire sauce, lemon juice, chili powder, mustard, and hot sauce. Stir constantly until the sauce comes to a simmer. Reduce the heat to low and cook for 45 minutes to 1 hour, stirring occasionally. Remove from the heat and let cool.

MAKE AHEAD:

The sauce will keep, covered, in the refrigerator for up to 2 weeks.

Alabama White Sauce

At many barbecue joints in the South this is the sauce of choice to accompany barbecued ribs, chicken, and pulled pork.

Makes about 1 cup

¾ cup mayonnaise

2 tablespoons cider vinegar

2 teaspoons prepared horseradish

Dash of Tabasco sauce

Kosher salt and freshly ground black pepper

Whisk together the mayonnaise, vinegar, horse-radish, Tabasco, and salt and pepper to taste in a bowl.

MAKE AHEAD:

The sauce will keep, covered, in the refrigerator for up to 2 weeks.

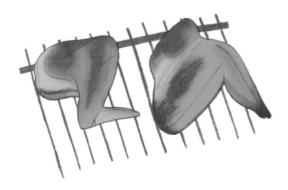

Cocktails & Drinks

Southern hospitality begins with a well-made cocktail to sip and savor. Whether you're making a classic mint julep or a Sazerac, or whipping up a batch of fresh peach Bellinis, these drinks are sure to get the party started.

✻✻✻✻✻✻✻✻✻✻✻

****

Simple Syrups

Homemade Lemonade

Raspberry Lemonade & Vodka

Iced Teas

Bloody Mary

Mint Julep

Sazerac

Watermelon Cosmo

Fresh Peach Bellinis

Bourbon & Orange Punch

Sparkling Ginger Punch

****

Simple Syrup

Simple syrup is a mixture of sugar and water that adds a sweet element to many cocktails. Most simple syrup recipes call for one part sugar to one part water, but feel free to experiment with different ratios to come up with your preferred version.

Makes about 1 cup

1 cup sugar

1 cup water

1. Put the sugar and water in a small saucepan and bring to a gentle boil over medium-high heat, stirring to dissolve the sugar. Reduce the heat to low and simmer, stirring occasionally, until the sugar is completely dissolved and the syrup is slightly thickened, about 3 minutes. Remove from the heat and let cool.

2. Transfer the syrup to a container with a tight-fitting lid, cover, and refrigerate until ready to use. The syrup will keep, covered, in the refrigerator for up to 3 or 4 weeks.

Simple Syrup Ratios

Thick Simple Syrup: 1 part water to 1 part sugar

Medium Simple Syrup: 2 parts water to 1 part sugar

Thin Simple Syrup: 3 parts water to 1 part sugar

Spiced Simple Syrup

Makes about 1 cup

1 cup sugar
1 cup water
2 cinnamon sticks
2 whole star anise
2 whole cloves
3 whole allspice berries

1. Put the sugar, water, cinnamon sticks, star anise, cloves, and allspice in a small saucepan and bring to a gentle boil over medium-high heat, stirring to dissolve the sugar. Reduce the heat to low and simmer, stirring occasionally, until the sugar is completely dissolved and the syrup is slightly thickened, about 3 minutes. Remove from the heat and let cool.

2. Strain the syrup into a container with a tight-fitting lid, cover, and refrigerate until ready to use. The syrup will keep, covered, in the refrigerator for up to 2 weeks.

Ginger Simple Syrup

Makes about 1 cup

1 cup of sugar
½ cup water
Four 1-inch pieces fresh ginger, trimmed and peeled

1. Put the sugar, water, and ginger in a small sauce-pan and bring to a gentle boil over medium-high heat, stirring to dissolve the sugar. Reduce the heat to low and simmer, stirring occasionally, until the sugar is completely dissolved and the syrup is slightly thickened, about 3 minutes. Remove from the heat and let cool.

2. Strain the syrup into a container with a tight-fitting lid, cover and refrigerate until ready to use. The syrup will keep, covered, in the refrigerator for up to 2 weeks.

Homemade Lemonade

Homemade lemonade is so much better than store-bought or frozen. Keep a pitcher of it on hand in the refrigerator—to drink on its own or to use as a base for any number of thirst-quenching drinks.

Makes about 1½ quarts

5 to 6 lemons

4 cups cold water

¾ cup Simple Syrup (page 60)

Squeeze enough lemons to make 1 cup of fresh lemon juice. Transfer to a large container or pitcher. Add the water and syrup, stir well and refrigerate until cold.

Raspberry Lemonade & Vodka

Fresh raspberries are a wonderful addition to lemonade. Simply purée and strain the berries and stir. For a lovely summer refresher, serve it with a shot of vodka over a tall glass of ice.

Serves 6

½ pound fresh raspberries, plus more for serving

1 quart Homemade Lemonade (see above)

6 ounces vodka

Lemon wedges, for serving

Fresh mint sprigs, for serving

1. Put the raspberries in a blender and blend until smooth. Strain the mixture through a fine sieve into a bowl by pressing a ladle against the strainer in a circular motion. Add the raspberry purée to the lemonade and stir well.

2. Fill 6 tall glasses with ice and add 1 ounce of vodka to each glass. Fill each glass with the raspberry lemonade and stir. Garnish with the lemon wedges, whole raspberries, and mint sprigs, and serve.

MAKE AHEAD:
The raspberry lemonade will keep, covered, in the refrigerator for 3 days. Stir well before serving.

Iced Tea

Iced tea is made for leisurely sipping, so it's no wonder that it's a favorite drink of the South. A pitcher of iced tea will keep in the refrigerator for a few days, so it's a good idea to make a batch for thirsty friends who may drop by.

For a delightful cocktail, fill a highball glass with ice and add 1 ounce of vodka, gin, bourbon, or whiskey. Add the iced tea and gently stir. Garnish the drink with a lemon slice, a sprig of mint, or any other garnish of your choice.

Southern Sweet Tea

Sweet tea is one of the South's iconic beverages, and it is always served at luncheons, family suppers, and parties. A pinch of baking soda is the key ingredient to making sweet tea—it cuts the bitterness and makes the tea very clear.

Makes 2 quarts;
serves 6 to 8

Pinch of baking soda
6 tea bags
¾ cup sugar
6 cups cold water

1. Bring 2 cups of water to a boil. Sprinkle the baking soda into a 2-quart, heatproof pitcher or container with a lid. Add the boiling water and tea bags. Cover and let stand for 15 minutes.

2. Remove the tea bags and discard. Add the sugar and stir until dissolved. Add the cold water and refrigerate until cold.

MAKE AHEAD:
The sweet tea will keep, covered, in the refrigerator for up to 1 week.

Iced Mint & Lemon Verbena Tea

Lemon verbena lends an aromatic citrus flavor to mint tea and a touch of honey adds just the right amount of sweetness.

Makes 2 quarts; serves 6 to 8

2 quarts of water

2 tablespoons mint tea leaves

1 tablespoon plus 1 teaspoon honey

8 sprigs lemon verbena

Lemon slices, for garnish

1. Bring the water to a boil in a large saucepan over high heat. Add the tea and remove the pan from the heat. Cover and let stand for 5 minutes. Add the honey and stir until dissolved. Add the lemon verbena sprigs and let stand for 5 more minutes.

2. Strain the tea into a pitcher and let cool, then chill in the refrigerator. Serve over ice in chilled glasses, garnished with the lemon slices.

Iced Strawberry & Lemon Tea

Take full advantage of fresh-picked strawberries in season to garnish your iced tea.

Makes 2 quarts; serves 6 to 8

2 quarts of water

2 tablespoons plus 2 teaspoons strawberry tea leaves

½ cup sugar

Juice of 1 lemon

3 large strawberries, sliced, for garnish

Lemon slices, for garnish

1. Bring the water to a boil in a large saucepan over high heat. Add the tea, sugar, and lemon juice, and remove the pan from the heat. Cover and let stand for 5 minutes. Stir gently to make sure the sugar is dissolved. Let stand for 5 minutes longer.

2. Strain the tea into a pitcher and let cool, then chill in the refrigerator. Serve over ice in chilled glasses, garnished with the strawberries and lemon slices.

Bloody Mary

The Bloody Mary has long been a favorite of weekend brunch-goers and is considered to be a great hangover remedy. But don't think of it only as a brunch beverage—Bloody Marys are fantastic to serve at a cocktail party, especially with oysters on the half shell or shrimp cocktail. Try this version garnished with spears of pickled okra.

Serves 6

1 bottle (46 ounces) tomato juice

2 tablespoons fresh lemon juice

2 tablespoons fresh lime juice

2 tablespoons prepared horseradish

1 tablespoon hot sauce

1 tablespoon Worcestershire sauce

Dash of celery salt

Freshly ground black pepper

6 ounces vodka

Celery ribs, for garnish

Lemon wedges, for garnish

Pickled okra spears, for garnish

1. Combine the tomato juice, lemon and lime juice, horseradish, hot sauce, Worcestershire sauce, celery salt, and pepper to taste in a large container with a tight-fitting lid. Cover tightly and shake vigorously. Refrigerate for at least 2 hours or up to 2 days. Shake well before using.

2. Fill 6 rocks glasses with ice and add 1 ounce of vodka to each glass. Fill the glasses with the Bloody Mary mixture and stir. Garnish each drink with a celery rib, lemon wedge, and pickled okra spear, and serve.

Mint Julep

The official cocktail of the Kentucky Derby is the mint julep, and the key to making this quintessential Southern cocktail is to use good bourbon and very fresh mint. Although you can make a mint julep in a highball glass, it somehow tastes better when it's sipped from a chilled silver julep cup.

Makes 1 drink

2 sprigs of fresh mint

½ ounce Simple Syrup (page 60) or 1 teaspoon of sugar

2 ounces bourbon

Crushed ice

In the bottom of a highball glass or a chilled julep cup, gently muddle one sprig of mint with the simple syrup or sugar. Add 1 ounce of the bourbon and fill halfway with crushed ice. Stir with a long spoon until the outside of the glass frosts. Add the remaining 1 ounce bourbon and more crushed ice to fill the glass. Stir again to frost, garnish with the remaining mint sprig, and serve.

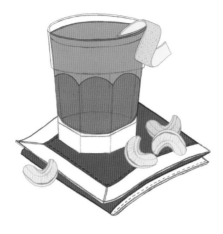

Sazerac

The Sazerac is a vintage New Orleans drink that pairs well with rich cocktail snacks such as Southern-Style Deviled Eggs (page 16) or Crab Cake Sliders (page 40). If you love a good whiskey cocktail, especially one that's topped off with a dash of bitters, the Sazerac is for you.

Makes 1 drink

Splash of Herbsaint

2 ounces rye whiskey

½ ounce Simple Syrup (page 60)

2 dashes Peychaud's bitters

Lemon or orange peel, for garnish

Chill 1 rocks glass while preparing the drink in another rocks glass. Splash the Herbsaint into the second glass and swirl it, then pour it out. Add the rye, syrup, and bitters to the glass and stir with an ice cube to chill. Strain into the chilled rocks glass. Garnish with a lemon or orange peel and serve.

Watermelon Cosmo

What could be more refreshing than a drink made with chilled watermelon juice? Just blend chunks of ripe seedless watermelon, fresh lime, and simple syrup together and you will have delicious juice to add to a drink like this fruity cosmo.

Makes 1 drink

Watermelon Juice:

1 small ripe seedless watermelon (about 6 pounds)

Juice of 1 lime

½ ounce Simple Syrup (page 60)

1½ ounces vodka

1 ounce triple sec

½ ounce fresh lime juice

2 ounces chilled watermelon juice

6 mint leaves

Lime slice, for garnish

1. To make the watermelon juice: Cut the watermelon in half and scoop chunks of the flesh into a blender. Discard the rind. Blend the watermelon until it is totally pulverized, about 1 minute. Add the lime juice and syrup and blend for a few seconds. Strain the juice, if desired, transfer to a pitcher and chill for at least 2 hours. Stir the juice with a long spoon if it becomes separated.

2. Fill a cocktail shaker with ice and add the vodka, triple sec, lime juice, watermelon juice, and mint. Shake well and strain into a martini glass. Garnish with a lime slice and serve.

Fresh Peach Bellinis

Fresh peaches grow in abundance in the South, where they have a long growing season. Juicy, fresh-picked peaches are the perfect fruit to use when making these lovely Bellinis.

Serves 6

3 very ripe peaches, peeled, pitted, and cut into chunks

1 tablespoon fresh lemon juice

1 ounce Simple Syrup (page 60)

1 bottle (750 ml) prosecco, well chilled

1. Put the peaches, lemon juice, and syrup in blender and blend until very smooth. Strain the mixture into a pitcher and chill in the refrigerator. Stir well before serving.

2. To serve, fill 6 champagne flutes about half-full with the peach juice. Top off with prosecco, stir gently, and serve.

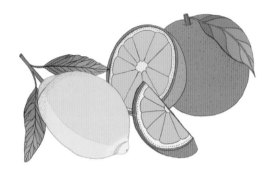

Bourbon & Orange Punch

A big bowl of punch is a beautiful and festive centerpiece for any party, and since it can serve a large number of guests, mixing one up can make your advance prep much easier. A good punch should be balanced and refreshing— not too sweet or fruity and not overly spiked with alcohol.

Serves 12 to 14

¾ **cup Spiced Simple Syrup (page 61)**

3 cups fresh orange juice

1 cup bourbon

1 bottle (12 ounces) ginger beer

1 bottle (12 ounces) seltzer or club soda

1 orange, thinly sliced, for garnish

1 lemon, thinly sliced, for garnish

1. Pour the syrup into a large pitcher. Add the orange juice and bourbon and stir to combine. Cover and refrigerate for at least 4 hours or overnight.

2. Pour the mixture into a punch bowl filled with ice and stir well to blend. Add the ginger beer and seltzer and mix gently. Float the orange and lemon slices on top and serve.

Sparkling Ginger Punch

All of the ingredients of this punch should be served very cold, so plan ahead and make sure that they are well chilled.

Serves 12 to 14

1½ cups Ginger Syrup (page 61)

1 cup fresh lime juice

2 (750 ml) bottles sparkling wine, chilled

2 limes, thinly sliced, for garnish

1. Pour the syrup into a large pitcher. Add the lime juice and stir to combine. Cover and refrigerate for at least 4 hours or overnight.

2. Pour the mixture into a punch bowl filled with ice and stir well to blend. Add the sparkling wine and mix gently. Float the lime slices on top and serve.

Index